NATIONAL
GEOGRAPHIC

A Cat's Whiskers

Sharon Street

Look at this cat.
A cat is built to take care of itself.

3

A cat feels things with its whiskers. A cat's whiskers help the cat know if it can fit through small spaces.

Did you know that whiskers help a cat feel its way in the dark?

A cat hears with its two ears.
A cat's ears can turn different ways
at the same time.

Did you know that a cat can turn just one ear towards a sound?
This helps the cat hear without turning its head.

A cat smells with its nose.
A cat's nose helps it recognize
people and places.

Did you know that a cat's sense of smell
is better than its eyesight?
Its sense of smell helps the cat
find safe places.

A cat sees with its two eyes.
A cat can see well when it is almost dark.

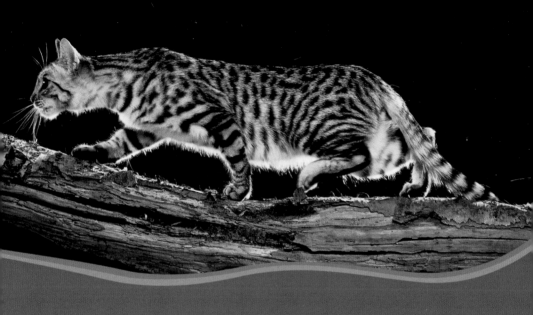

Did you know that a cat's eyes can see very small movements? This helps the cat when it is hunting.

A cat walks on its four paws.
A cat's paws have soft pads on the bottom.

Did you know that the pads on a cat's feet
help the cat to move quietly?
This helps the cat sneak up on prey.

A cat has a long, thin tail.
A cat's tail helps the cat keep its balance.

Did you know
that if a cat falls,
it moves its tail
and twists its body?
This helps the cat
to land on its feet.

What is this cat doing to take care
of itself?